Weird Pet Stories

Look for other

titles:

World's Weirdest Critters
Creepy Stuff
Odd-inary People
Amazing Escapes
Bizarre Bugs
World's Weirdest Gadgets
Blasts from the Past
Awesome Animals
Weird Science
X-traordinary X-tremes
Strange School Stories

Weird Pet Stories

by Mary Packard

and the Editors of Ripley Entertainment Inc.

illustrations by Ron Zalme

SCHOLASTIC INC.

New York   Toronto   London   Auckland   Sydney

Mexico City   New Delhi   Hong Kong   Buenos Aires

Contents

Introduction .1

Chapter 1
Extra-odd-inary Pets 5

Chapter 2
Totally Pet-culiar! 21

Chapter 3
Pampered Pets 37

Chapter 4
Smart and Talented 53

Chapter 5
Really Nice Saves 63

Pop Quiz 75

Answer Key 79

Ripley's Scorecard 83

Photo Credits 86

Developed by Nancy Hall, Inc.
Designed by R studio T
Cover design by Atif Toor
Photo research by Sharon Lennon

ISBN 0-439-68778-0

12 11 10 9 8 7 6   6 7 8 9/0

Printed in the U.S.A.
First printing, November 2004

Weird Pet Stories

Doggone Purr-fect

No one was more famous in the 1930s and '40s than Robert Ripley, creator of Believe It or Not! People flocked to his odditoriums—museums of the bizarre—to see such oddities as shrunken heads, "the human owl," and a two-headed calf. Thousands tuned in to Ripley's radio show and, at the height of his popularity, no fewer than 80 million readers marveled at his cartoons.

The first to admit he got some of his best ideas from his fans, Ripley received 3,500 letters a day, many of which were about some pretty amazing pets.

For example, who could forget the cat owned by A. W. Mitchell of Vancouver, British Columbia, that nursed orphaned chicks, or the rooster owned by O. J. Plomesen of Luverne, Minnesota, that pulled a carriage containing Plomesen's baby daughter down Main Street during parades?

A study done at the State University of New York at Buffalo concluded that the sounds of *meow, bow-wow,* and possibly *tweet-tweet* from pets may relieve someone's stress even more than comforting words from a human loved one. The reason? Pets are nonjudgmental and give their owners unconditional love. Other findings included the facts that heart attack survival rates are higher for pet owners, and that elderly patients who have pets need to see a doctor less often than those who don't.

Given what great companions pets make, it should come as no surprise that people may have been calling,

"Here, kitty, kitty," as far back as 9,000 years ago. When archaeologists uncovered a prehistoric village on the island of Cyprus, they found a grave—with the skeleton of a cat lying right beside the human remains! Scientists believe this proves that cats were domesticated 5,000 years earlier than was first thought.

In *Weird Pet Stories,* you'll read about such extraordinary animals as a kitten with two faces, a tree-climbing dachshund, and a fortune-telling horse, as well as find out the latest in high-fashion pet clothes, yoga for dogs, and much, much more. At the end of each chapter, you can test your animal smarts with the How Pet-culiar! quizzes and Brain Busters. When you're finished, take the special Pop Quiz at the end of the book to earn extra credit and add up your scores to find out your Ripley's rank. Get ready to be amazed at some pretty unbelievable pets and the incredible things they—and their owners—can do!

Believe It!®

Extra-odd-inary Pets

From tarantulas and alpacas to two-faced kittens and two-legged dogs, the world is filled with all kinds of unusual pets!

Little Miss Muffet:

Andrea Kendall of Athens, Georgia, used to suffer from arachnophobia, the fear of spiders. Deciding to conquer her fear in a big way, she bought a tarantula. Sure enough, Kendall learned to love the hairy creature and, before long, had ten of them. She says tarantulas make ideal pets because they don't take up much space and feel soft and silky to the touch.

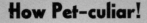

How Pet-culiar!

The reported number of people who have died after being bitten by any one of the 800 species of tarantula is . . .

a. 5,021.
b. 257.
c. 1,203.
d. zero.

Lizard Mania: If you visit Henry Lizardlover (yes, that's his real name—he changed it from Henry Schiff in 1986), you shouldn't be surprised to find a 12-year-old iguana named Prince Charming snoozing on the top shelf of his bedroom closet. Keep going, and you'll find 30 or more lizards sunbathing in a window-filled room in the back of his Los Angeles house. Living with so many iguanas, Lizardlover is perhaps the world's foremost authority on their nature and suitability as pets. He admits that iguanas are not ideal pets for most people because they grow very big and can be aggressive during breeding season. However, for those willing to take the time, he says they "have a perfect inner calm and trust just like you see in people." Lizardlover has parlayed his hobby into a thriving business, publishing a line of cards that feature the iguanas in humanlike poses. He and his unusual pets have also appeared on TV and in magazines.

How Pet-culiar!

Author Alexandre Dumas (1824–1895) drew many stares as he walked through the streets of Paris, France, with his pet . . .

a. crocodile on a leash.
b. boa constrictor around his neck.
c. raccoon on his shoulder.
d. vulture on a leash.

Cock-eyed! In 2002, four-inch-long Madagascar hissing cockroaches were trendy pets in Thailand. And why not? The big bugs are easy to care for, eat just about anything, and make a cool hissing noise when they're handled. Even after the roaches were banned as a possible health hazard, people continued to smuggle them into the country. In May

2003, officials seized about 1,000 of the illegal bugs and cremated them at a local dump. Then they held a traditional public funeral for the roaches!

Leash Law: It's against the law to walk a pet snake on a leash through public parks in Osnago, a town in northern Italy. Snake walking had become a growing trend there until the town's mayor decided that the fad was too dangerous.

Double Your Pleasure: If you're thinking of getting an alpaca, think twice—as in two are better than one. Alpacas are herd animals. Without the company of other alpacas, a single alpaca will become lonely and depressed. That's why these sociable creatures should always be purchased in pairs. Add that to the cost—a pregnant female alpaca can go for as much as $25,000—and you'd think they wouldn't be popular pets. You'd be wrong. The demand for these sweet-natured, affectionate animals has raised their number in the United States from about 1,000 in 1997 to 50,000 in 2004.

How Pet-culiar!

After losing 20 sheep to coyotes in just one year, Michael Riding got a new security guard, Ping, a . . .

a. llama.
b. Siberian tiger.
c. yak.
d. Vietnamese potbellied pig.

Slime Time: For most of us, adopting a snail for a pet is not at the top of the list. Some people, however, do keep snails as pets and even train them. Carl Bramham has trained his snail, Archie, to compete in races. In July 1995, Archie won the annual World Snail Racing Championship held in Congham, Norfolk, England, beating out 150 other snails and setting a world record. The speedy snail took a mere two minutes and 20 seconds to race from the middle of a 13-inch circle to its outside edge.

Bright Idea: There's something fishy going on at Yorktown Technologies in Texas. Their newest product has everyone seeing red. That's because they have just been licensed to sell GloFish, the first genetically engineered pet. Developed by

Zhiyuan Gong at the National University of Singapore, GloFish glow red in the dark! By extracting a gene from a sea coral and implanting it in a zebra fish, Gong first developed GloFish as a way to detect toxins in the environment. Now GloFish are poised to become the latest fad in pets!

Ear-y! Can you imagine having a rat as a pet? Rat breeder Steffany Heller of Harrisburg, Pennsylvania, usually has at least 75 rats in her home at any given time. In 1999, even her seven-month-old daughter, Teagan, was partial to Socrates, a five-month-old dumbo rat,  whose large, low-set ears and broad head give it a cuter look than its domestic relatives.

Big Guy: At 48 inches from the tip of his nose to the tip of his tail, Leo, a male Maine coon cat owned by Frieda Ireland and Carroll Damron of Chicago, Illinois, is about three times the size of an average house cat. Leo eats a normal diet, but once in a while he gets to eat his favorite treat—blue cheese.

Earning His Stripes: People can't be blamed for pointing and staring at Robert Merkel. After all, it's not every day that you see someone driving a car around with a 900-pound tiger as a passenger. Merkel has permission from the state of Florida to keep the tiger, whose name is Rajah. His neighbors in Dania Beach don't seem to mind. In fact, some report that they enjoy waking up to the sound of Rajah's roar. Owning a tiger is legal in Florida as long as the animal is well cared for and regularly used for educational or commercial purposes.

Prairie Pets: Prairie dogs imported from Texas and Oklahoma are popular pets in Japan.

How Pet-culiar!

Rat expert Debbie Ducommun has a Web site devoted to . . .

a. recipes for making home-cooked dinners for rats.
b. patterns for knitting the latest in rat fashions.
c. how to breed rats.
d. how to brush a rat's teeth without getting bitten.

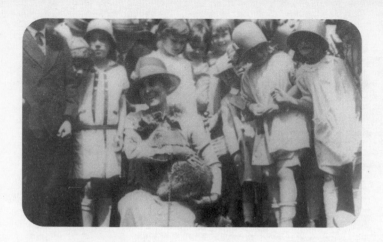

Merry Menageries: The families of Presidents Theodore Roosevelt (1858–1919) and Calvin Coolidge (1872–1933) had more pets in the White House than any other presidents. In addition to dogs and cats, the Roosevelt pets included snakes, horses, horned toads, a macaw, and several guinea pigs. The Coolidges had 12 dogs, two cats, several birds, a bobcat, a lion cub, a wallaby, a bear, and a 500-pound pygmy hippopotamus! Above, Grace Coolidge shows off their pet raccoon to children at the 1927 Easter egg rolling on the White House grounds.

What a Hoot! British nurse Florence Nightingale (1820–1910), who is considered the founder of modern nursing, always carried a pet owl in her pocket.

Monkey Business: Alex, a pet gibbon, boarded a flight from Phoenix, Arizona, to Minneapolis, Minnesota, and sat in a full-fare seat—and no one noticed until lunch was served!

Technical Problems: When Professor Kevin Warwick, head of cybernetics at England's Reading University, wanted to take his 4-foot-long robotic cat to Moscow, Russia, in 1999, he was refused a seat by British Airways on the grounds that animals are not allowed to travel in the cabin. Warwick tried to explain that his "cat" wasn't a live animal, but the airline didn't get it. Luckily, the Russian airline, Aeroflot, did, and Warwick and his robotic companion finally made it to their destination.

How Pet-culiar!

When Jaroslav Kana takes his pet for a walk in a Czech park, other animals shy away from his . . .

a. wolf.
b. tiger.
c. lion.
d. puma.

Taking a Stand:

A collie–spaniel pup owned by A. A. Rankin of Puyallup, Washington, was born without hips or hind legs, but it could stand on its two front legs and run almost as fast as any of its four-legged friends.

Heads Up! Ten-year-old Hunter York of Centertown, Kentucky, found his latest pet in his own backyard. When he picked up the black king snake with a stick, he was amazed to find that it had two heads! Luckily, king snakes do not hurt humans, but they do eat poisonous rattlesnakes and copperheads.

York named the snake Mary-Kate and Ashley and hopes that it might have a future in show business.

Double Image: You'd have to go pretty far to find another cat like Image, who was born in June 2000 in Bensalem, Pennsylvania. Her owner, Sandra Pyatt, said she didn't notice that Image was different from her littermates until her 12-year-old son, Timothy, called it to her attention. Image was different all right. She had one head, but two faces! Because both faces are controlled by one brain, Image yawns with both mouths, sneezes with both noses, and blinks with all four eyes simultaneously.

How Pet-culiar!

Among dogs, a Lhasa apso owned by Angela Barrett of Bellville, Ontario, Canada, holds the record for having the . . .

a. longest tongue (12 inches long).
b. smallest feet (one-half inch long).
c. longest tail (36 inches long).
d. longest eyelashes (3.5 inches long).

Getting Around: Veronica Brelsford's German shepherd, Sam, had trouble getting around because of arthritis in his hind legs. In 2001, Eddie's Wheels for Pets, a company in Shelburne, Massachusetts, fitted him out with a "wheelchair," and Sam is mobile once again.

Wheelie Adorable: In August 2000, when a three-week-old stray kitten that had been born without a pelvic bone, was dropped off at a veterinary clinic in Lancaster, Pennsylvania, Dr. Edwin Jeszenka and his staff adopted him and named him Speedy. Since nothing could be done medically for the kitten, Jezsenka designed a tiny "wheelchair" that his office manager, Linda Steinmetz, built out of K'NEX toy parts. After just one day of practice, Speedy was barreling around the office like a pro.

How Pet-culiar!

To make these animals sound more appealing, pet store owners have taken to marketing giant cockroaches as . . .

a. doodle bugs.
b. rain beetles.
c. buggy-wuggies.
d. cock-a-doodles.

Toe-tally Amazing:

Mooch, a cat from Oakland, Maine, is the proud owner of 28 claws. That's ten more claws than most cats have. Though Mooch has to walk with his legs spread apart so he doesn't trip over his own big feet, sometimes they come in handy. When walking on snow, Mooch's feet work like snowshoes, keeping him from sinking in. Luckily for the other cats and dogs in the neighborhood, Mooch never uses his claws on them. His owner, Becky Duval, says that her big-footed cat is a lover not a fighter.

Two's Company:

Noël Daniels of Wellington, South Africa, who was watching his pet tortoise's eggs hatch,

thought he was seeing double when a two-headed baby stepped out of its shell. Despite its two heads, this rare tortoise turned out to be healthy in every way. The heads take turns eating, and sometimes one sleeps while the other is awake, but both seem to get along with each other just fine.

The Better to Smell With: A Llewellin setter, raised by John E. Glenn of Benton, Arkansas, was born with two noses—and was the envy of hounds for miles around.

The Better to Hear You: Mr. Jeffries, a bassett hound owned by Phil Jeffries, of West Sussex, England, doesn't have any trouble hearing, but he does occasionally get tripped up by his ears—which are insured for $48,000. Why? Because at 11.5 inches long, Mr. Jeffries's ears are the longest recorded ears of any dog in the world. Believe It!

How Pet-culiar!

Studies have found that introducing children to pets at a very young age can . . .

a. result in the syndrome known as petophobia.
b. help prevent allergies.
c. cause asthma.
d. result in delayed speech.

Robert Ripley believed that truth is often stranger than fiction—and when it comes to pets and their owners, he couldn't have been more right!

Robert Ripley dedicated his life to seeking out the bizarre and unusual. Yet every unbelievable thing he recorded was proven to be true. In the Brain Buster at the end of every chapter, you'll play Ripley's role—trying to verify the fantastic facts presented. Each Ripley's Brain Buster contains a group of four shocking statements. Of these so-called "facts," **one** is **fiction**. Will you **Believe It!** or **Not!**?

Wait—there's more! Following the Brain Busters are special bonus questions where you can earn extra points! Keep score by flipping to the end of the book for the answer key and a scorecard.

Pets are true to their owners, but only three of the wacky facts below are true. Can you spot which fact is totally false or will you be barking up the wrong tree?

a. In the May 2004 issue of the *Psychological Science* magazine, a researcher reported that many people choose pets that look like themselves.

Believe It!   **Not!**

b. Toto, a dog owned by Roland Frank of Hamilton, Michigan, gave birth to one puppy on April 3, 1970, then had four more pups 30 days later.

Believe It!   Not!

c. The pygmy terrier is a breed of dog that grows no bigger than an adult human's thumb.

Believe It!   Not!

d. White cats with one blue eye and one green eye are often deaf.

Believe It!   Not!

• •

BONUS QUESTION

Despite the fact that it's among the deadliest animals in the world, one of the most popular pets in Bangkok, Thailand, is the . . .

a. beaked sea snake.

b. blue-ringed octopus.

c. golden poison-dart frog.

d. Sydney funnel-web spider.

Pets are capable of doing some of the strangest things—but then, so are the humans who love them!

Wacky Rabbit:

One sizzling summer day, Hobie the rabbit was hot—so hot that he was panting. His owner felt sorry for Hobie, so he filled a half-barrel with water and put the rabbit in it to cool him off. To his amazement, Hobie could actually float on his back. What's more, the rabbit seemed to be enjoying himself. Now Hobie takes a dip in the barrel every day, and his owner says it's almost impossible to coax him out!

How Pet-culiar!

Tessa, a bull terrior owned by Johan Van Graan of South Africa, adopted and nursed three orphaned . . .

a. hyenas.
b. warthogs.
c. lion cubs.
d. jack rabbits.

Scuba Kitty:

Most cats would do anything to keep from getting wet— but not a certain calico named Hawkeye. One day, Hawkeye, who lives in Reading, California, surprised her owner, Gene Alba, when she jumped into the pool and paddled alongside him as he did his laps. That made Alba wonder if Hawkeye might like to go scuba diving with him as well. So he rigged up a one-of-a-kind kitty diving outfit composed of a harness, an oxygen tank, and breathing apparatus. Hawkeye jumped right in, and now she stays down with Alba for an hour at a time. Alba says his feline companion seems to feel relaxed underwater.

Cat-ching a Wave: Ted Townsend of Ormond Beach, Florida, regularly takes his pet cat, Toby, surfing!

Up a Tree:

Charles McClain is the proud owner of Tree Cat, a real-life scaredy-cat. McClain found the cat three years ago, crying from a perch high in a 60-foot-tall oak tree. McClain tried everything to coax him down, but Tree Cat wouldn't budge. Now, McClain gets up at six o'clock every morning and climbs a ladder to give the cat his breakfast. This routine suits Tree Cat just fine, because he still hasn't left the tree! Tree Cat has it made in the shade with his own custom-made home, complete with a soft bed, a front porch, and a deck where he eats his meals.

How Pet-culiar!

Gypsy, a dog owned by Preston Cathcart, asks for food by . . .

a. jumping up on the kitchen table and barking.
b. distinctly saying, "I want some."
c. lying in front of the refrigerator with her tongue hanging out.
d. sitting up on a chair and begging.

Signing Canine:
Nicki Arndt of Colorado communicates with her deaf dog, Annie, by using sign language.

Big Mouth: Augie, a golden retriever owned by Lauren Miller of Texas, can pick up and hold five balls in his mouth at once. (The fifth ball is behind the two balls in the front.)

Paws and Fins: Chester the chimpanzee enjoyed water-skiing while being pulled by a dolphin!

Brave Hearts

Up start: This brave pup could run almost as fast as its four-legged friends, despite having no hips or hind legs.

Hot Stuff! Scarlet the cat risked her life by running into a burning building to rescue her five kittens, one at a time. Luckily, Scarlet recovered from her burns, and she and her kittens all found new homes.

Wheel Help: Eddie's Wheels for Pets, a company in Shelburne, Massachusetts, makes "wheelchairs" for pets that have trouble getting around. This German shepherd, named Sam, suffers from arthritis in his hind legs.

Silly Pet Tricks

From Trees to Skis: Twiggy the squirrel jets across the pool on skis while her owner operates the miniature boat pulling her by remote control.

Bird Brain: When Crackers the parrot doesn't feel like spreading his wings, he jumps on his scooter and takes off!

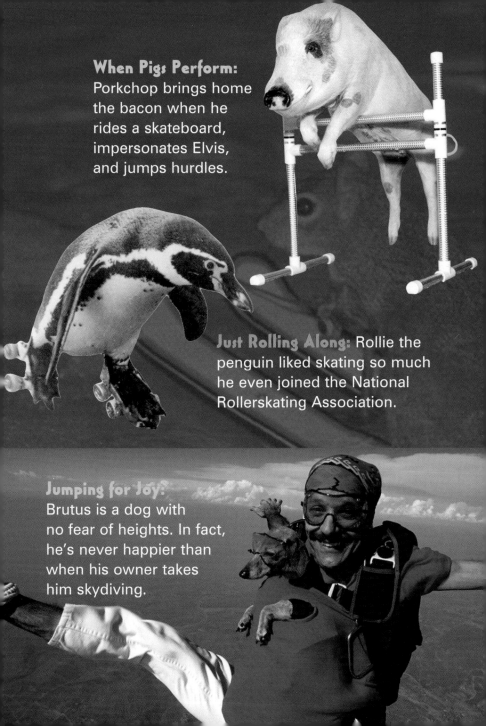

When Pigs Perform: Porkchop brings home the bacon when he rides a skateboard, impersonates Elvis, and jumps hurdles.

Just Rolling Along: Rollie the penguin liked skating so much he even joined the National Rollerskating Association.

Jumping for Joy: Brutus is a dog with no fear of heights. In fact, he's never happier than when his owner takes him skydiving.

Odd-inary Pets

Leapin' Lizards: Prince Charming, one of Henry Lizardlover's 30 iguanas, gives his pal Tallulah a ride on his bike.

Slime Time: Carl Bramham not only keeps snails as pets, but also trains them to compete in races. Archie, his most-prized racer, holds the record as the world's fastest snail!

Getting Rat-tled: At the age of seven months, Teagan, the daughter of rat breeder Steffany Heller, loved to play with Socrates, a five-month-old dumbo rat.

Arachnophobia: It took buying a tarantula for Andrea Kendall to conquer her fear of spiders. Now she keeps ten tarantulas as pets.

Glow Figure! Get ready to meet the first designer pets. Called GloFish, these flashy zebra fish have been genetically engineered to be the same fluorescent red color as a sea coral.

Made in

Catwalk for Canines: Eight dogs, dressed in the latest fashions, strutted their stuff down the catwalk at a fashion show sponsored by the Mitsukoshi Department Store in Tokyo, Japan.

Pampered Pooches: Pet Tents of Omaha, Nebraska, caters to pets that like to sleep in—the house, that is. Your pet is sure to have sweet dreams sleeping on the comfy buckwheat cushion inside the billowing white mesh of the Midsummer Night's Dream House.

The Cat's Meow: Dressed to the nines in her best formal hat and gown, Didi beat 200 other cats to win the grand prize in a competition that took place in Kuala Lumpur in 2003.

the Shade

How Fortunate!

To ensure that their pets will continue to live in the style to which they've grown accustomed, some wealthy pet owners leave their money to their pets when they die. In 2002, Tinker the cat inherited the equivalent of $937,000 from her deceased owner.

Watch the Birdie!

Thanks to FlightSuits, reusable diapers for birds from Avian Fashions in Virginia, pet owners can dress up their birds and let them out of the cage without having to worry about messy accidents.

SPARE PARTS

Beside Itself: Noël Daniels's two-headed tortoise has two brains, so it's not unusual to catch one head napping while the other one is awake!

Two-faced: No, you're not seeing double. Image the kitten was born with one head but two faces! Since Image has just one brain, both faces blink, yawn, and sneeze at the same time.

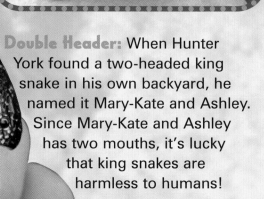

Double Header: When Hunter York found a two-headed king snake in his own backyard, he named it Mary-Kate and Ashley. Since Mary-Kate and Ashley has two mouths, it's lucky that king snakes are harmless to humans!

What a Croak!

With the help of hypnosis, Bill Steed taught his frogs many skills, including weight lifting.

Roller Days: Rollie the penguin was a member of the National Roller Skating Association.

How Pet-culiar!

Every year, animals compete in such events as the long jump, weight lifting, and a rope climb when Nebraska Wesleyan University hosts the . . .

a. Event Formerly Known as the Rat Olympics.
b. Daredevil Dog and Playful Pony Show.
c. Calaveras County Fair & Jumping Frog Jubilee.
d. World Chicken Festival.

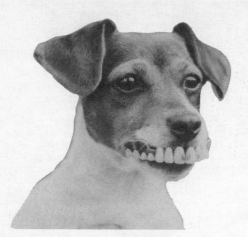

Smile!
A dog owned by Mrs. W. R. Rhodes liked to wear her owner's false teeth.

Purr-fect Performance: In 1999, Lobster, a three-year-old cat owned by Lesli Van Shack of Charlotte, North Carolina, was crowned "Best Singing Cat" at the Advantage Search for North America's Best Singing Pet in New York City, beating contestants from all over the United States and Canada. The contest was sponsored by Advantage, a company that makes flea-control products for pets. Van Shack says Lobster has always loved to sing. Her prize-winning performance? Meowing along to "Stray Cat Strut" by the Stray Cats.

Grand Cat: The grand-prize winner of a cat competition in Kuala Lumpur on July 20, 2003, was a cat from Malaysia named Didi. Formally dressed in a hat and gown, she was chosen from more than 200 other cats dressed from head to paw in their very best.

Mental Floss: A cockatoo named Rikki, doesn't have any teeth, but she apparently thinks she does. After watching her owner, Donna Felsing, floss each morning, Rikki decided it looked like fun. So she picked up a box of dental floss, broke off a piece, and pulled it though her beak with her claws. Felsing says Rikki will do anything for attention, and now will floss her beak on command.

How Pet-culiar!

In the Inner Mongolia region of China, people stage beauty contests for their . . .

a. camels.
b. horses.
c. yaks.
d. goats.

Cat Burglar: In the middle of the night, Juniper Polos of Queens, New York, gets up from a 16-hour nap, and goes to work. Juniper doesn't have a regular job, like an investment banker or stockbroker. No, Juniper is (literally) a cat burglar. Wary neighbors have learned not to leave their laundry on the clothesline overnight because those who forget are likely to find that their underwear, a sock, or a favorite T-shirt has vanished without a trace. Beach towels and toys left outside are other particular favorites of Juniper's. Once the sun rises and Juniper's shift ends, he convinces neighbors to feed him by meowing outside their windows at the top of his lungs. Afterward, Juniper returns home to his owner, Dave Polos, stashes his loot, eats more breakfast, and takes another 16-hour nap. After all, being a cat burglar is hard work!

How Pet-culiar!

A Jack Russell terrier named Zipper keeps his owner company by riding . . .

a. in the passenger seat of his motorycycle.
b. on a bodyboard while he's swimming.
c. on the handlebars of his mountain bike.
d. on a snowboard while he's skiing.

Best Dog: In 1995, Dan Anderson and Lori Chapasko fell in love while volunteering at a Wisconsin animal shelter. That's why Anderson thought it would be fitting to propose to Chapasko at the shelter and later,

have Samson, his six-year-old Samoyed mixed-breed dog, serve as best man at their wedding.

Purr-fect Eti-cat: When Tessa the cat eats, she uses a fork. It all started when Faye Murrell's grown children left the family nest. The dinner table seemed very empty without them. So Faye showed Tessa how to behave at

the dinner table. The clever cat learned how to use a fork in no time. Now she eats with Faye and her husband. When noodles are served, Tessa chows down with chopsticks, and on special occasions, she eats ice cream with a spoon.

Watertight: In 1998, Dan Heath of Medford, Oregon, could barely believe his eyes when he saw, Chino, his golden retriever, standing over a fishpond, nose to nose with Falstaff, an orange-and-black carp. Each day, Chino sprints out to the backyard, peers into the water, and waits. Within seconds, Falstaff pops up and the two gently touch noses. Heath doesn't know how or why Chino and Falstaff became friends, but it's obvious to anyone who sees them that their friendship is watertight!

Rolling Along: When Betty Ottaviano observed her daughter's stroller moving across the floor by itself, she thought her house was haunted. A closer look revealed that it was actually her pet box turtle, Nikki, who was propelling it forward. She gave Nikki a treat for its effort, and now the turtle pushes the stroller whenever it wants a snack.

Weather Cat: In the 1930s, a cat named Napoleon became a well-known celebrity. Why? For his skill at predicting the weather. It all started during a drought in 1930. Weather forecasters in Baltimore, Maryland, were predicting more dry weather when Frances Shields called to report that it definitely was going to rain by the following day. When asked how she came by her information, Shields replied that Napoleon was lying down with his "front paw extended and his head on the floor," something he did only if it was going to rain soon. The reporters laughed and brushed Shields off. When it rained the next day, however, they changed their tune. From then on, Napoleon's weather predictions appeared daily and—Believe It or Not!—he was right just as often as the professional forecasters!

How Pet-culiar!

When a dog stands still and stares, with its tail raised and its mouth closed, it is . . .

a. saying, "Let's play."
b. relaxed and alert.
c. terrified.
d. sending a warning signal to back off.

Most Faithful Companion: When the three o'clock train pulled into Japan's Shibuya station, an Akita dog named Hachi was always there, waiting to walk home with his master, Eisaburo Ueno, who was a professor at Tokyo University. Then on May 21, 1925, Ueno

didn't get off the train. It turned out that he had died while he was at work. Relatives adopted Hachi, but the dog kept returning to his old home and going to meet the train. The stationmaster and others began to feed and care for Hachi, who continued to meet the train until he died in 1935. After Hachi's story made the newspapers, people from all over Japan sent donations to build a statue of him at the station. Though the statue was melted down during World War II, it was rebuilt in 1948 and has since become a landmark.

How Pet-culiar!

Dainty Doris, a 1,300-pound Holstein cow in Ontario, Canada, . . .

a. goes skateboarding.
b. goes downhill skiing.
c. pulls children on a sled.
d. carries a calico cat around on her back.

Lots of 'Tude: Brutus is a dog with both attitude and altitude. Once he gets an idea in his head, this miniature dachshund is like, well, a dog with a bone. His owner, skydiver Ron Sirull, couldn't get Brutus to stop chasing his plane down the runway.

So Sirull finally gave in and on May 1, 1997, he tucked the little dog into a pouch on his chest and took him skydiving. Now Brutus is a pro, with more than 100 jumps under his collar.

All Aboard! No one knows why, but it's not unusual for dogs to step onto commuter trains and take a seat! One such dog did exactly that on Christmas Eve of 2003. Passengers on Metro-North say the mixed-breed spaniel–retriever boarded somewhere along the line in Connecticut and was finally collared in Harlem, New

York. Authorities were hoping to find his owner, but even if they didn't, the dog would still have a home. Since he was featured in the news, countless offers to adopt him flooded in.

Up a Tree: In 1998, a Lakewood, Colorado, animal control officer thought she'd heard wrong when she got a call asking for help getting a dog down from a tree. She hadn't. Joey the dachshund had climbed almost to the top of a 35-foot-tall blue spruce. With the help of a cherry picker, Joey was returned to the ground. His owners, Jamie and Clancy King, said Joey had been known to climb trees before while in hot pursuit of squirrels and cats.

How Pet-culiar!

Hambone, a potbellied pig owned by Philip and Ruth Dillener of Woodridge, Virginia, can play . . .

a. crazy eights.
b. badminton.
c. croquet.
d. a musical keyboard.

Pets can perform some pretty incredible feats, but only three of the accomplishments described below are true. Can you tell which one is just plain hogwash?

a. Lisa Carney of Whitefish, Montana, taught her jackrabbit, Bonny, how to hold a potato peeler so she could scrape her own carrots.
Believe It!   Not!

b. Johnny Blaiser of Coyle, Oklahoma, taught his quarter horse, Ice, how to fish by holding a rod and reel in her mouth.
Believe It!   Not!

c. At the Columbus Days' Pet Show in 2001, Trudy, a box turtle, one of the pets in a therapy program at the Columbus Public Schools in Ohio, took first place in the pet tricks division for jumping through a hoop.
Believe It!   Not!

d. In the 1950s, Sammy, the firehouse cat at Fire Station Six in Long Beach, California, would slide down the brass pole with his crew at the first sound of the fire alarm.
Believe It!   Not!

BONUS QUESTION

When Private James Brown of England was sent to France to fight in World War I, he was soon followed overseas and found in the trenches by his loyal pet . . .

a. homing pigeon, Seeker.

b. cat, Josephine.

c. dog, Prince.

d. parrot, Pollyanna.

When it comes to loving, honoring, and spoiling pets— the sky is the limit.

High Style: For pets that like a little fantasy in their lives, Pet Tents of Omaha, Nebraska, sells fanciful pet beds, such as the Midsummer Night's Dream House for $174.95. For seriously pampered pooches, Le Chien in New York offers the ultimate in high-style pet accessories, such as jasmine- and tuberose-scented perfume for $45 a bottle, and a faux mink coat and carrier for $695. Need some new doggy furniture? Dining tables start at $300, sofas at $410—and for the ultimate in pet beds, you can get Le Chien's Bed Royale for a mere $2,500!

How Pet-culiar!

The automatic punishment for anyone who deliberately killed a cat in ancient Egypt was . . .

a. death.
b. 30 lashes with a cat-o'-nine-tails.
c. exile.
d. 30 years of slavery.

Home Sweet Home: The Pet Professor, Inc., in Calgary, Alberta, Canada, plans to hold a Doggie Dream Home contest to celebrate the 100th anniversary of the Alberta Kennel Club. They've even created their own deluxe doghouse based on the Parthenon, a temple in Greece.

Nice Duds: At Barks Pup Avenue in Lithia, Florida, you'll find clothes in a variety of sizes to suit all kinds of dogs. For males, you can purchase baseball, football, and hockey jerseys that celebrate your favorite team. For females, you'll find a large selection of dresses, ranging from a Hawaiian muumuu to holiday party dresses. For that special occasion, you might want to get your dog a leather coat trimmed with sheared beaver and lined with sheepskin from Chic Doggy in New York.

How Pet-culiar!

Pop singer Christina Aguilera takes her dogs to a pet . . .

a. spa featuring mud baths.
b. ranch featuring a bone-shaped swimming pool.
c. disco.
d. restaurant where pets are served gourmet meals in gold-rimmed bowls.

On the Fly: Attention, bird lovers! Now you can let your pet bird fly around the house all day without having to worry about messy accidents dirtying the furniture. Avian Fashions in Virginia has come out with FlightSuits, reusable diapers for birds! Want to dress your bird up? The company also offers costumes ranging from Birdie Bunny (complete with bunny ears) and Feather Witch (with matching FlightSuit) to Tux with Tails (top hat sold separately).

Chowing Down: Ginger, a spaniel owned by Harold Calvert of Burnt Hills, New York, has her own credit card—with a $10,000 limit— that she uses to buy dog food.

Puppy Love:
Tatiana Anjelica and Tyson Beckford were married on June 2, 2003, in Derby, Connecticut. With tails wagging and dressed to the teeth, the dogs could barely

contain their excitement as they shared a wedding cake made out of dog food and cheese snacks. The groom wore a top hat and tuxedo while the bride wore a veil and a tiny garter on her paw. Ten of their best canine pals shared in the festivities.

Cat-chy Idea: If your feline companion is taking too many catnaps, and her only reaction to her cat toys is a big, fat yawn, *Meow TV* may be just what the doctor ordered. Sponsored by Meow Mix, *Meow TV* bills itself as a "show for cats and the people they tolerate." With videos of squirrels and fish, and segments such as "Kitty Yoga" and "Cat Haiku," *Meow TV* is guaranteed to put an end to kitty boredom forever.

How Pet-culiar!

Scientist Hans-Rainer Kurtz of Hanover, Germany, was the first to pioneer . . .

a. contact lenses for pets.
b. organ transplants for pets.
c. a permanent wave for long-haired cats and dogs.
d. a hearing aid for cats.

Party Dog: In 1991, Robert Wolley of New Jersey paid $1,000 for a birthday party for his dog, Jeb, that included a concert performed by an orchestra and a grooming session with a complimentary bathrobe.

A Feast for Fido:

For New Year's Eve 2004, a department store in Japan sold a specially packaged New Year's meal just for dogs. The meal included 30 tasty dishes, guaranteed to set a dog's tail to wagging. The price? A mere $273!

Doggy Paddle:

After a broken leg ended his soccer career, Craig Harrison of Northumberland, England, opened the Four Paws Hydrotherapy Centre for overweight dogs. Instead of spending two hours a day walking their dogs, busy people can now give their pooches the same amount of exercise by stopping at the pool for half an hour. Just one minute of swimming in the special pool equals walking a full mile!

Mush, Doggy! Dog scootering is the latest in canine sports. Owners simply harness their dogs to a scooter, hop on, and off they go. Dogs love to run, so they really enjoy their exercise—and those people who love their dogs but are not so fond of exercise get a real lift!

Dog Days: Is your dog stressed? If so, you might consider taking him or her to a Ruff Yoga class. Students do all the traditional poses, but with a twist—their dogs are incorporated into the moves.

How Pet-culiar!

A Web site for dogs in Great Britain features pictures of . . .

a. fire hydrants.
b. cats.
c. dogs in cars.
d. dogs playing Frisbee.

Pet-icure: In Ibusuki, Japan, pets, as well as people, are frequently wrapped in thick sponges or kimonos and buried in the hot volcanic sands to improve their circulation and general health.

Preventing Cat-astrophes: For all those softhearted pet owners who can't bring themselves to banish feline friends from the computer room, PawSense is just the thing. This ingenious software can distinguish between the typing

patterns of humans and cats. After it detects a feline on the keyboard, PawSense makes a noise that will annoy the cat enough to make it flee. In addition, the software immediately blocks any keyboard input from the cat, so owners will no longer have to worry about a pet erasing the fruits of their labor.

Dot.Tom Cat: When Rachel Hawkwood, cofounder of Web retailer Intersaver.co.uk, was just getting started, she brought her kitten, Ziggy, to work with her. Ziggy's pleasing personality went a long way to calm the start-up jitters that plagued the staff. In fact, Ziggy became such an important part of the office routine that she was given her own shares in the company.

How Pet-culiar!

Virgin Atlantic Airways has introduced a pet plan that offers jet-set pets . . .

a. gourmet meals.
b. in-flight grooming services.
c. a special in-cabin section where they can play or take a nap in a pet bed.
d. frequent flyer miles.

Ticket to Ride: Owney, a mongrel dog that was the mascot of the Albany, New York, Post Office from 1888 to 1897, was the first dog to travel around the world alone, making the journey in 132 days. Traveling by himself on the United States Post Office Railway Mail Service, Owney journeyed 143,000 miles

in nine years and collected 1,107 post office baggage tokens from the places he visited.

Not Lost in Translation: Pet owners have always known that cat vocalizations are meaningful. Now, Takara, a Japanese toy company, has developed a palm-sized electronic device called Meowlingual to take the

guesswork out of interpreting a favorite feline companion's meows and growls. The cat no longer has to wait in frustration for its owner to figure out what it wants. With Meowlingual, the instant gratification it deserves is at hand.

Shady Characters: When MidKnight, Ken and Roni Di Lullo's Labrador retriever–border collie mix, began missing Frisbee shots because he was blinded by the sun, the Di Lullos came up with a solution. They made a pair of strap-on sunglasses for him. So many dog owners wanted a pair that they named the glasses Doggles and began to sell them. Now more than 50,000 dogs are sporting Doggles—and no doubt their Frisbee games have improved as much as MidKnight's did!

I'm Home! The problem with the average pet door is that the occasional chipmunk or squirrel just might come waltzing into the house. Now, instead of a pet door, you can try a new product, the Pet-2-Ring Doorbell. The device comes with a video showing owners how to use food rewards to train their pets to push a lever—which rings inside the house. Then owners know that their pet is waiting by the door, ready to come inside.

How Sweet It Is!

For those who like to get up close and personal with their pets, a new product is about to sweeten the experience. With odor-fighting ingredients such as green-tea extract and rosemary oil, Pit'r Pat breath fresheners promise

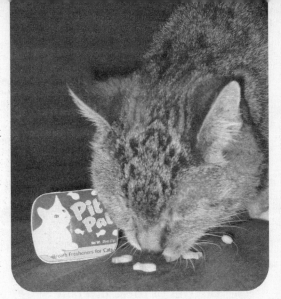

to banish kitty breath—at least for a little while. Yip Yap Mints will do the same thing for dogs.

How Pet-culiar!

A Pekingese dog who was crowned supreme champion at Crufts, England's most famous dog show, may be stripped of his title because . . .

a. his owner may have bribed one of the judges.
b. he might have had a secret facelift.
c. he wore fake fur extensions.
d. he hadn't had all of his shots.

Flavor of the Day:

If you don't want your dog to drink untreated water, try the bottled water offered by K9 Water Company. It comes in four flavors: Gutter Water (beef), Toilet Water (chicken), Puddle Water (liver), and Hose Water (lamb).

R-eel-y over the Top:

Lucius Crassus (140–91 B.C.E.), a Roman authority on the law, was so fond of his trained lamprey eel that he gave it earrings and a pearl necklace. When the fish died, Crassus wore mourning clothes for an entire year!

Doggone! For years, a mixed-breed pit bull named Pig had the run of the University of Texas at Austin, attending classes with students and acting as mascot at

varsity athletic events. When Pig was hit by a car in 1923, his body lay in state at the Co-Op, where hundreds of mourners came to pay their respects, and afterward, take part in the funeral procession, which was led by the Longhorn Band. "Taps" was played at the burial site and a marker was left with the epitaph: PIG'S DEAD . . . DOG GONE.

Pet Heirs: Some pets continue to be pampered even after their owner's death. When tobacco company heiress Doris Duke died in 1993, she left $100,000 to her dog. In 1999, singer Dusty Springfield died and left her cat, Nicholas,

to a friend in England along with enough money for a lifetime supply of the cat's favorite treat—imported baby food from the United States. When Margaret Layne of London, England, died in 2002, she left her entire estate, valued at the equivalent of $937,000, to her cat, Tinker, a former stray.

Faithful and Trusting: In the United States, 17 states have laws allowing pet owners to set up trust funds in their wills to provide for their pets after they die. The cost to set up the trust fund is about $2,000, and, according to *Lawyers Weekly USA*, the average amount of money bequeathed to a pet is $25,000.

How Pet-culiar!

In 1891, the Squire of Flying Hall in North Yorkshire, England, built a giant pigsty in the shape of . . .

a. a Greek temple.
b. an Egyptian pyramid.
c. Windsor Castle.
d. the Eiffel Tower.

Dog Worship Day:

In October 2003, trainers at the Nepal Police Dog Training School in Kathmandu worshipped their trainees before posing them for a group portrait. On the second day of the annual five-day-long Tihar Festival, Nepalese Hindus pray to dogs to guard their houses and keep them from destruction, as well as to show their respect and give thanks to the animals that have faithfully served them.

Don't Mess:

Myobu No Omoto, a cat owned by the Japanese emperor Ichijo, was so well loved that a dog that chased it was exiled, and the dog's attendant was put in jail.

How Pet-culiar!

Horses pulling tourists in carriages around the streets of Vienna, Austria, are required to wear . . .

a. padded horseshoes to keep the noise down.
b. heavy fur blankets to keep them warm in the winter.
c. sunglasses to protect their eyes from the sun.
d. diapers to keep the streets clean of manure.

By now, you've probably figured out that pet owners will go to almost any lengths to keep their animals happy. Almost, that is. Three of the four facts below are true, but one should give you pause. Can you spot the "fact" that's a real howler?

a. When they're away from home, 40 percent of the pet owners in the United States call on the phone to let their pets hear the sound of their voices.

Believe It!   **Not!**

b. The InterPet, marketed by a company called Pet Tech in Saginaw, Michigan, is a computer that makes it possible for dogs and cats to order their favorite foods with the touch of a paw.

Believe It!   **Not!**

c. A gas station in Herefordshire, England, has set up an automatic dogwash, where pets can be shampooed, rinsed, and blown dry.

Believe It!   **Not!**

d. At the Malibu Pet Hotel, pampered pets can stay in air-conditioned private rooms or a furnished two-bedroom apartment and, during their stay, enjoy long daily walks, grooming, and lots of chew toys.

Believe It!   **Not!**

BONUS QUESTION

In 2003, the cost of the services and supplies pet owners in the United States bought for their animals added up to a grand total of . . .

a. 18 million dollars.

b. 105 million dollars.

c. 31 billion dollars.

d. 1.2 trillion dollars.

Some pets are not only devoted and faithful companions to their humans but also intelligent and talented animals!

Not Horsing Around: In the 1920s, a horse named Lucky Wonder used its nose to type out psychic predictions. Lucky predicted that President Harry Truman would be reelected and that the United States would fight in World War II.

How Pet-culiar!

English sheepdogs can . . .

a. be trained to jump over 6-foot-high fences.
b. train their own offspring to guard sheep.
c. be guided by hand signals from as far as a mile away.
d. run faster than greyhounds.

No Way! Ashley Whippet, a champion Frisbee dog, once leaped so high that he grabbed a Frisbee from the crossbar of a football goalpost.

Well Balanced: Tim, a horse owned by J. D. Winton of Australia, could balance his entire weight on one small wooden block while his rider stood up in the saddle, twirling a lasso.

Pig-casso: Since he first picked up a brush in 1998, Smithfield, a Vietnamese potbellied pig, has produced paintings so lovely that they've fetched hundreds of dollars apiece on eBay. To date, through the sale of his art, the productive pig has earned $20,000, all of which has been donated to charities.

How Pet-culiar!

Isaac, a golden retriever that belongs to Gary Wimer, can . . .

a. load and unload the dishwasher.
b. add, subtract, multiply, divide, and do square roots.
c. withdraw money from an ATM.
d. use a telephone.

Trunk Show: In 1854, a British animal trainer named Cooke taught two circus elephants to sit at a table, use giant forks to eat dinner, and sip wine from oversized goblets.

Whole Hog: Have you ever seen a skateboarding pig? Not lately? Well, a pig named Porkchop likes to ride one now and then—with another pig supplying the elbow—or perhaps we should say

bacon—grease. In fact, the pusher's name is Bacon. Porkchop and Bacon can also do more than 100 other tricks, including shooting hoops and tooting horns.

On a Roll: Peppy, a Dalmatian belonging to professional "birler" Bill Fontana of Fort Frances, Ontario, Canada, could roll a log for an entire mile in an hour's time.

She's the Best!

After they adopted a baby squirrel that had fallen out of its nest, Chuck and Lou Ann Best found they had their hands full. Their new pet, named Twiggy,

was getting into everything! *Maybe she's bored*, they thought. The Bests loved to water-ski, so they decided to let Twiggy try the sport. They made her a pair of tiny skis and fastened her to a remote-controlled toy motorboat. Each time Twiggy completed a lap around the pool, she got a treat. Since then, the Bests have adopted other abandoned baby squirrels and taught them to water-ski. Now the Best squirrels are on the road, performing at boat shows and on TV.

How Pet-culiar!

Jana Edmondson of Santa Rosa, California, has trained her dog, Stock, to . . .

a. wash his paws by dipping them in a basin of water before entering the house.
b. recognize and respond to 15 words written on flash cards.
c. read road signs.
d. walk to the store and buy a newspaper.

Rock and Bull Story:

A pit bull terrier named Pete earns $20 a day by barking in time to the music of the rock band PJ and the Magic Bus.

Doggone Amazing: Skidboot was an adorable puppy with some terrible habits— like chasing the neighbors' chickens and chewing up everything in sight. One day his owner, David Hartwig of Quinlan, Texas, decided to teach his dog some manners. Skidboot learned the new behaviors so fast, Hartwig thought he was a genius. Hartwig wasn't the only one. Now Skidboot wows rodeo and TV audiences all over the country. He even has his own book and video. In one trick, Skidboot holds a biscuit between his teeth while Hartwig reads the ingredients listed on the package—and Skidboot doesn't chomp down on the biscuit until he hears the word *beef*!

Little Chatterbox: Puck, a parakeet owned by Camille Jordan of Petaluma, California, had a vocabulary of 1,728 words when it died in 1994.

No Way! In 1938, a popular attraction at the State Fair of Texas was Captain E. C. Lower's Bozo, the Mind-Reading Dog. Bozo could accurately bark out the number, dates, and denominations of coins held in audience members' hands, the number of rings on their fingers, and any number his master was thinking.

Role-Playing: The dog that played the first Lassie in the 1943 film *Lassie Come Home* was a male dog named Pal. In fact, every dog that ever starred as Lassie in the movies or on TV was a male dog—even though Lassie was supposed to be a female!

How Pet-culiar!

Portuguese water dogs were kept aboard some ships of the Spanish Armada to . . .

a. keep the ships free of vermin.
b. keep the crew company.
c. warn the crew when enemy ships approached.
d. swim from ship to ship carrying messages.

Out of the Trenches: In 1918, Corporal Lee Duncan rescued a German shepherd puppy from a bombed-out kennel in France. He named the dog Rin Tin Tin, after finger puppets that French children gave to American soldiers for good luck. When the war ended, Duncan took the puppy home to California, where they made the rounds of the Hollywood movie studios. Rin Tin Tin made his debut in the 1922 silent film, *The Man from Hell's River,* and went on to star in 25 more movies for Warner Brothers. Rin Tin Tin earned $6,000 per month, was insured for $100,000, and had his own chauffeured limousine, as well as his own cook and valet. Though the original Rin Tin Tin died in 1932, his relatives carried on his legacy in both movies and television.

How Pet-culiar!

Louise, a 250-pound wild boar, has been trained by German police to . . .

a. act as a security guard at the Berlin Central Police Station.
b. chase down and capture fleeing criminals.
c. direct traffic.
d. root out hidden drugs that even dogs can't find.

Ripley's Believe It or Not! Brain Buster

Pets may be smarter and more talented than you thought, but only you can ferret out which three facts below are true and which one is just a cock-and-bull story!

a. When a stolen parrot in New Delhi, India, was brought to court as a witness, it identified its real owner by repeating the names of her children.

Believe It!   **Not!**

b. Using his nose as a cue stick, Tuffy, a toy poodle owned by Cap and Joyce Goldsmith, could clear all the balls on a billiard table in less than a minute.

Believe It!   **Not!**

c. At Pennsylvania State University, Professor Stanley Curtis taught six pigs to play video games by using their snouts to control the joy sticks.

Believe It!   **Not!**

d. After a home owned by Jason Black of Clearwater, Florida, was burglarized, Black's dog, Kento, correctly identified the suspect from his photograph in a book of mug shots.

Believe It!   **Not!**

BONUS QUESTION

In 1910, Paris art critics gave high praise to an artist named Boronali for his painting, *Sunset on the Adriatic Sea*. Only later did they learn that Boronali was . . .

a. a donkey who painted with a brush tied to his tail.

b. a dolphin who held the paintbrush in her mouth.

c. a dog who used her claws and teeth to create the painting.

d. an elephant who painted with the tip of his trunk.

The following close calls prove two things: that truth can be stranger than fiction and that heroes come in a variety of shapes, sizes, and species.

Hot Dog! In 1936, a firehouse dog named Blackie saved a cat from a burning building by carrying it down a ladder.

How Pet-culiar!

Jake, a 12-week-old puppy, survived after swallowing a . . .

a. diamond necklace.
b. 12-inch-long carving knife.
c. tuning fork.
d. pack of razor blades.

Little Squealer: When a restaurant owner in New York City was murdered by a customer on July 12, 1942, his pet green parrot told police the name of the killer. The bird had been taught to identify patrons by name, so when the parrot kept repeating the same name over and over, the police knew they had their man!

Bull Session: Donald Mottram of Carmarthen, West Wales, owes his life to his favorite cow, Daisy. In 1966, Mottram was in his pasture when he was attacked by a 3,000-pound bull. The snorting beast charged, knocked Mottram to the ground, and stomped on him. The farmer lost consciousness. An hour and a half later, a dazed Mottram awoke to find that his herd of cows had formed a protective ring around him. Led by Daisy, they continued to shield him from the bull as he crawled away to safety.

How Pet-culiar!

When actor Drew Barrymore's house caught fire, she was able to save herself after being awakened by . . .

a. ET, her parrot.
b. Ming, her Persian cat.
c. Beep, her guinea pig.
d. Flossie, her mixed-breed dog.

Mighty Rat: Fido the rat was sleeping peacefully when he was awakened by the smell of smoke. He broke out of his cage and scampered through flames and up the stairs to where Lisa Gumbley and her daughters, nine-year-old Megan and three-year-old Shannon, were sleeping. Fido scratched and scratched at their door, refusing to leave until they awoke. Happily, the family escaped without injury, but if it hadn't been for Fido, mother and daughters surely would have perished in the fire.

The Cat's Meow:

When a lamb wandered away from a farm in Gloucestershire, England, and accidentally fell into a swimming pool, a cat named Puss Puss saw it happen. She started meowing at the top of her lungs and dashing back and forth from the pool to the garden where her owners were working. Puss Puss kept it up until they followed her to the pool. The lamb was discovered in the nick of time, and Puss Puss was pronounced a hero.

Earning Her Stripes:

Sometimes animals raised in captivity lose their natural instincts. That happened in 2001 at a zoo in Uzbekistan when a Siberian tiger rejected her own cub. Luckily, a stray dog named Klava had more than her share of motherly love to go around. Klava nursed the tiger cub for 30 days, until it was strong enough to switch to a diet of meat. Without Klava's care, the baby, a member of an endangered species, most certainly would have died.

Fish Out of Water: When retired ambulance driver Leo van Aert of Belgium saw his pet carp floating on its side, he did what he was trained to do—he gave the fish a heart massage. As soon as the carp began to move again, van Aert returned it to the water. The fish swam around for a while, but then it stopped moving again. This time, van Aert gave the fish mouth-to-mouth resuscitation. That seemed to do the trick, and the carp has been doing swimmingly ever since!

Vacuum-Packed:

A seven-week-old kitten was sleeping in a pile of leaves in Melbourne, Australia, when a street-cleaning machine came along and vacuumed it up. Alerted by frantic

meows, the driver stopped the machine, but by the time he got the kitten out, it was only semiconscious. Luckily, the driver was able to revive the kitten by blowing into its nose to inflate its lungs. Then he took the kitten to a veterinarian, who was amazed that such a little cat could survive such a big ordeal. The kitten has since been adopted and named Hoover.

Polar Pony:

In 1821, Ferdinand Von Wrangel was leading a Russian expedition to Siberia when his horse plunged through the ice on the Dogdo River. The horse stayed in the frigid water for several hours, until he was finally rescued by a group of Siberians who used long poles to lift him out.

How Pet-culiar!

Flossie, a sheepdog in Denmark, survived for . . .

a. 68 days trapped inside a dry well.
b. two weeks buried under earthquake rubble.
c. three days trapped beneath an avalanche.
d. seven days at sea after being washed overboard in a storm.

Cat Among the Chickens:
Frowsy, a cat owned by the Mitchells of Vancouver, British Columbia, Canada, raised several orphaned chicks as her own offspring.

Eight Lives to Go: As workers doing renovations in Stefanie Winkler's apartment finished walling up a fireplace in a rarely used guest room, they failed to notice that Winkler's kitten, Lily, had gotten inside. Winkler didn't know where Lily had gone—until she entered the room more than three weeks later and heard meows coming from inside the wall. A neighbor helped Winkler free the kitten from the wall, alive but extremely hungry!

Atomic Kittens: In February 1996, a pregnant cat snuck onto the grounds of the closed San Onofre nuclear power plant in San Diego, California, had a litter of kittens, and then disappeared. A worker found four tiny black orphans, but when she tried to leave with them, the plant's alarms went off, frightening people for miles around. It turned out the kittens, now called Alpha, Beta,

Gamma, and Neutron, were slightly radioactive. The incident made headlines, and people from all over the world wanted to adopt the cats, but workers at the power plant had first dibs. Seven months later, the kittens were pronounced "radiation free," prompting the owners of the power plant to use them in a pronuclear public relations campaign.

How Pet-culiar!

When a woman in Hermitage, Tennessee, fell and cut her head, her niece came to the rescue after being alerted by the woman's pet . . .

a. iguana.
b. monkey.
c. cat.
d. canary.

Cat Care: When it comes to bravery, you'd have to go far to find a cat like Scarlet, who was named by her caregivers because of the raw, red burns all over her body. Scarlet got the wounds by dashing through flames into a burning building in Brooklyn, New York—not once, but five times—once for each of her kittens. When the

story was broadcast on radio and television, hundreds of people offered to adopt the mother and her kittens. Now all six have found loving homes.

Not in Plane Sight: Meani, a cat on a Northwest Airlines flight from Albuquerque, New Mexico, to Nashville, Tennessee, was reported missing when workers went to transfer his carrier to a connecting flight at the Minneapolis - St. Paul International Airport. The little escape artist was spotted in a baggage handling area. Efforts to capture him failed—until someone opened a can of tuna. After his meal, Meani was put on a flight and returned to his owner.

Yum! Veterinarians in Moscow, Russia, were able to save the life of a hamster after it had been swallowed whole by a dog.

Laundry Lesson: Two-year-old Laura Jones of Manchester, England, thought her kitten could use a little sprucing up. Since she'd seen her mother get the gray out of dirty clothes by throwing them in the washing machine, Laura figured the same method should work for a gray kitten. So into the washing machine went Simba, along with a bunch of socks and underwear. It's a good thing Laura's five-year-old brother spied the soggy little thing swirling around in the washer and called their mother. She plucked the kitten out, gently dried her off, and whisked her off to the vet. Astonished that the kitten had survived, the vet pronounced her fit as a fiddle. Since then, Simba has not been seen anywhere near the laundry room!

How Pet-culiar!

A New Zealand teenager was rescued from a burning garage when his mother was alerted by . . .

a. the frantic barking of his German shepherd.
b. his cat repeatedly throwing herself against the garage door.
c. his parrot squawking "Fire!"
d. his pet kangaroo beating on the garage door with its tail.

Hoodwinked: Anyone who knows anything about cats knows that they are attracted to warm places—and what could be warmer than a freshly turned-off car engine? No doubt that's why a cat crawled up onto the engine of a parked car to take a snooze. Unaware of the napping cat, Alyson Preston, the car's owner, started it up and drove seven miles before discovering the frightened cat under the hood!

Good Boy! Robert Sinclair became critically ill while living in a remote farmhouse in Falkirk, Scotland. He was rescued after putting a note in a bottle and dropping it out of a window. His rescuer? A neighbor's border collie, who found the bottle and took it back home to his owners.

How Pet-culiar!

A cat named Lionel survived without food and only an occasional drink of rainwater for the two months it was trapped . . .

a. in a chimney.
b. in a debris-filled basement after the house burned down.
c. in a covered hot tub.
d. under earthquake rubble.

It may be a dog-eat-dog world out there, but not when it comes to pets rescuing people—or even other animals. Three of the heroic animal rescue stories below are true. Can you figure out which one is just a bunch of horsefeathers?

a. After Jack Fyfe of Sydney, Australia, had a stroke, his dog, Trixie, kept him alive for nine days until help arrived by bringing him water in a soaked towel.

Believe It! **Not!**

b. One cold, rainy night in 2003, Ivor Lunde's dachshund, Agathon, became a national hero in Norway when he led his owner down a rocky beach to a missing four-year-old child, who'd been trapped for hours on a slippery rock just offshore.

Believe It! **Not!**

c. Hundreds of cats owe their lives to Ginny, a dog owned by Philip Gonzalez of Brooklyn, New York, who rescues strays from Dumpsters, air-conditioning ducts, and other dangerous places.

Believe It! **Not!**

d. In 2004, a half-tame Siberian tiger owned by Ziggy Nestor of Vermilion, Ohio, raced into the waters of Lake Erie to rescue a drowning child.

Believe It! **Not!**

BONUS QUESTION

When two burglars forced their way into Rebecca Moyer's home, her screams were heard, and the crooks were frightened away by her valiant . . .

a. 10-pound cat, Tiger, who hurled herself at one of the bad guys, scratching and biting his face.

b. 300-pound pig, Arnold, who chomped on one of the bad guy's legs.

c. red-tailed hawk, Skye, who spread her wings to their full 42-inch wingspan and flew at the bad guys, slashing them with her talons.

d. 400-pound lion, Pussycat, who bounded into the room, bared his teeth, and let out a mighty roar.

POP QUIZ

You've read lots of wild facts about domestic animals. Now it's time to stop horsing around and get back in the ring. Take off the blinders and find out just how well you've trained your memory with this Pop Quiz. Will you gallop right through it? You won't know until you try!

1. Arachnophobia means fear of . . .
a. snakes.
b. spiders.
c. squirrels.
d. cats.

2. Yorktown Technologies in Texas has developed a brand-new type of fish that . . .
a. glows red in the dark.
b. is covered with fur.
c. jumps through hoops.
d. purrs when it's content.

3. Florence Nightingale, the founder of modern nursing, always carried in her pocket a pet . . .
a. tarantula.
b. mouse.
c. owl.
d. cockroach.

4. In the 1930s, a cat named Napoleon became a celebrity for his unique ability to . . .

a. walk a tightrope.

b. catch Frisbees.

c. play chess.

d. predict the weather.

5. A resident of Lakewood, Colorado, had to call animal control when his dachshund got stuck up in a tree.

Believe It!   Not!

6. The name of the cat who was crowned "Best Singing Cat" in a 1999 contest was . . .

a. Boca Grande.

b. Pipes.

c. Lobster.

d. Raindrop.

7. The latest product from Avian Fashion is . . .

a. mini sunglasses for birds.

b. feathered hats for cats.

c. feather capes for cats.

d. reusable diapers for birds.

8. PawSense is a device that . . .

a. protects computer keyboards from curious cats.

b. keeps pets from clawing the furniture.

c. discourages dogs from jumping on the furniture.

d. protects pets' paws from snow and ice.

9. Toilet Water, a new product for dogs, is actually . . .
a. perfume.
b. flavored bottled water.
c. scented shampoo.
d. furniture repellent.

10. Smithfield, a Vietnamese potbellied pig, achieved fame because . . .
a. of his artistic talent.
b. he saved his owner from drowning.
c. he chased burglars out of his owner's home.
d. of his ability to ride a skateboard.

11. In the 1920s, a psychic horse named Lucky Wonder accurately predicted the Vietnam War.
Believe It!   **Not!**

12. A squirrel named Twiggy is best known for her ability to . . .
a. ride a skateboard.
b. ice-skate.
c. water-ski.
d. roller-skate.

13. When David Hartwig of Quinlan, Texas, first took his puppy, Skidboot, home, he was amazed by how . . .
a. smart the puppy was.
b. well the puppy got along with his cattle.
c. high the puppy could jump.
d. much trouble the puppy managed to get himself into.

14. When a baby Siberian tiger at a zoo in Uzbekistan was rejected by her mother, she was adopted and nursed by Klava, a female gorilla.

Believe It!   **Not!**

15. When a restaurant owner in New York City was murdered by a customer, the killer was arrested because the victim's . . .

a. dog led police to the killer by following his scent.

b. pig clamped down on the killer's leg until the police arrived.

c. tiger sat on the killer until the police got there.

d. parrot repeated the killer's name to the police.

Answer Key

Chapter 1
Extra-odd-inary Pets
Page 5:   **d.** zero.

Page 6:   **d.** vulture on a leash.

Page 8:   **a.** llama.

Page 11:   **a.** recipes for making home-cooked dinners for rats.

Page 13:   **c.** lion.

Page 15:   **d.** longest eyelashes (3.5 inches long).

Page 16:   **b.** rain beetles.

Page 18:   **b.** help prevent allergies.

Brain Buster: **c.** is false.

Bonus Question: **b.** blue-ringed octopus.

Chapter 2
Totally Pet-culiar
Page 21:   **c.** lion cubs.

Page 23:   **b.** distinctly saying, "I want some."

Page 25:   **a.** Event Formerly Known as the Rat Olympics.

Page 27:   **a.** camels.

Page 28:   **b.** on a bodyboard while he's swimming.

Page 31:   **d.** sending a warning signal to back off.

Page 32:   **b.** goes downhill skiing.

Page 34:   **d.** a musical keyboard.

Brain Buster: **a.** is false.

Bonus Question: **c.** dog, Prince.

Chapter 3
Pampered Pets

Page 37:   **a.** death.
Page 38:   **b.** ranch featuring a bone-shaped
           swimming pool.
Page 40:   **d.** a hearing aid for cats.
Page 43:   **c.** dogs in cars.
Page 44:   **d.** frequent flyer miles.
Page 47:   **b.** he might have had a secret facelift.
Page 49:   **a.** a Greek temple.
Page 50:   **d.** diapers to keep the streets clean
           of manure.

Brain Buster: b. is false.
Bonus Question: c. 31 billion dollars.

Chapter 4
Smart and Talented

Page 53:   **c.** be guided by hand signals from as far as
           a mile away.
Page 55:   **b.** add, subtract, multiply, divide, and do
           square roots.
Page 57:   **b.** recognize and respond to 15 words written
           on flash cards.
Page 59:   **d.** swim from ship to ship carrying messages.
Page 60:   **d.** root out hidden drugs that even dogs
           can't find.

Brain Buster: d. is false.
Bonus Question: a. a donkey who painted with a brush
tied to his tail.

Chapter 5
Really Nice Saves

Page 63:   **b.** 12-inch-long carving knife.

Page 64:   **d.** Flossie, her mixed-breed dog.

Page 67:   **a.** 68 days trapped inside a dry well.

Page 69:   **d.** canary.

Page 71:   **b.** his cat repeatedly throwing herself against the garage door.

Page 72:   **c.** in a covered hot tub.

Brain Buster: d. is false.

Bonus Question: b. 300-pound pig, Arnold, who chomped on one of the bad guy's legs.

Pop Quiz

1. **b.**
2. **a.**
3. **c.**
4. **d.**
5. **Believe It!**
6. **c.**
7. **d.**
8. **a.**
9. **b.**
10. **a.**
11. **Not!**
12. **c.**
13. **d.**
14. **Not!**
15. **d.**

What's Your Ripley's Rank?

Ripley's Scorecard

Give yourself a pat on the back! You've boned up on your knowledge of pets and proven that you can tell fact from fiction. Now it's time to get your Ripley's rating. Are you **Taking a Catnap** or are you a **Top Dog**? Use this page to tally the trivia questions you answered correctly. Then add up your scores to find out how you rate.

Here's the scoring breakdown. Give yourself:
★ **10 points** for every **How Pet-culiar!** you answered correctly
★ **20 points** for every fiction you spotted in the **Ripley's Brain Busters**
★ **10 points** every time you fielded a **Bonus Question**
★ and **5 points** for every **Pop Quiz** question you got right.

Here's a tally sheet:

Number of **How Pet-culiar!**
questions answered correctly: _____ x 10 = _____
Number of **Ripley's Brain Buster**
fictions spotted: _____ x 20 = _____
Number of **Bonus Questions**
you fielded: _____ x 10 = _____
Number of **Pop Quiz** questions
answered correctly: _____ x 5 = _____

Final score: _____

0–100
Taking a Catnap?

That's okay. Maybe you don't have a pet or perhaps animals are just not your thing. No problem. There are lots of other Ripley's Believe It or Not! books with different topics that might open your eyes to the world of the strange and unusual. Do you like excitement? Try *X-traordinary X-tremes*. Is science your topic? Pick up a copy of *Weird Science*. And if you're the scholarly type, don't miss *Strange School Stories*!

101–250
You're No Birdbrain!

It's obvious you're not winging it! Without a doubt, you're starting to develop a taste like Robert Ripley's for the kind of weird and wacky facts about pets that fill this book. Keep flying right, and you'll soon be feathering your nest with your own weird pet stories!

251–400
Fin-tastic!

Congratulations! You're doing just swimmingly! It's true you didn't get every question right, but, hey! You're a fast learner. With just a bit more practice, you'll soon be fishing for unusual stories yourself and netting the place of Top Dog on the Ripley's scorecard.

401–575
Top Dog!

Give yourself a treat! You certainly have a scent-sational nose for sniffing out unbelievable facts about pets! Robert Ripley would definitely be proud of you! Now that you've finished *Weird Pet Stories*, you're probably sitting up and begging for more strange and unusual facts to bone up on. Well, you won't have long to wait. More new Ripley's Believe It or Not! books will be coming your way soon!

Believe It!®

Photo Credits

Ripley Entertainment Inc. and the editors of this book wish to thank the following photographers, agents, and other individuals for permission to use and reprint the following photographs in this book. Any photographs included in this book that are not acknowledged below are property of the Ripley Archives. Great effort has been made to obtain permission from the owners of all materials included in this book. Any errors that may have been made are unintentional and will gladly be corrected in future printings if notice is sent to Ripley Entertainment Inc., 7576 Kingspointe Parkway, Suite 188, Orlando, Florida 32819.

Black & White Photos

6 Prince Charming and Tallulah/Henry Lizardlover

8 Alpacas/AP Photo/*The Times-Standard*/ Michael Hughes

10 Teagan Heller and Socrates/AP Photo/*Patriot-News*/Gary Dwight Miller

12 Grace Coolidge/Library of Congress, Prints & Photographs Division

16 Veronica Brelsford and Sam/AP Photo/Matthew Cavanaugh

27 Didi/AP Photo/EPA/Ahmad Yusni

28 Juniper/David Polos

30 Chino and Falstaff/AP Photo/*Mail Tribune*/Bob Pennell

37 Pet Tent/Courtesy of The Persnickety Pet

39 Cockatoo/Courtesy of www.bird-diaper.com

40 Tatiana Anjelica and Tyson Beckford/AP Photo/*Connecticut Post*/Brian A. Pounds

43 Yoga Class/AP Photo/Dianne Bondareff

45 Cat and Meowlingual/AP Photo

46 Dog Wearing Doggles/Courtesy of Doggles/Zebra Publishing

47 Cat with Pit'r Pat/L. C. Casterline

49 Cat Wearing Crown/Getty Images/Stone

50 Nepal Police Dog Trainees/AP Photo/EPA/Narendra Shrestha

55 Smithfield/AP Photo/*The Richmond Times-Dispatch*/Lindy Keast Rodman

58 Skidboot/Courtesy of www.skidboot.com

64 Parrot/Ablestock

66 Klava and Siberian Tiger Cub/AP Photo

70 Scarlet and Her Owner/Courtesy of North Shore Animal League

71 Hamster/PhotoDisc

Color Insert

(1) Scarlet and Her Owner/Courtesy of North Shore Animal League; Veronica Brelsford and Sam/AP Photo/Matthew Cavanaugh

(2-3) Twiggy the Squirrel/Newscom; Crackers the Parrot, Porkchop the Pig/www.tophogs.com; Brutus the Skydiving Dog/Aerialfocus.com/Tom Anders

(4-5) Prince Charming and Tallulah/Henry Lizardlover; Snail/Getty Images/Brand X Pictures; Teagan Heller and Socrates/AP Photo/*Patriot-News*/Gary Dwight Miller; Tarantula/Ablestock; GloFish/AP Photo/Ed Wray

(6-7) Dog Fashion Model/Reuters; Pet Tent/Courtesy of The Persnickety Pet; Didi/AP Photo/EPA/Ahmad Yusni; Cat Wearing Crown/Getty Images/Stone; Hippie Bird/Mike Morones/The Free Lance-Star

(8) Two-headed Tortoise/AP Photo/Obed Zilwa; Two-faced Kitten/AP Photo/*Courier Times*/Jay Crawford; Two-headed Snake/AP Photo/*The Messenger-Inquirer*/John Dunham

Cover

Prince Charming and Tallulah/Henry Lizardlover; Tarantula/Ablestock